I AM SUCCESSFUL

5 KEYS TO WINNING IN BUSINESS

Dr. Barbara A. Palmer

I AM SUCCESSFUL
5 KEYS TO WINNING IN BUSINESS

Kingdom Publishing, LLC
1350 Blair Dr., Odenton, MD 21113

Printed in the United States of America (USA)

ISBN: 978-1-967006-06-9

TABLE OF CONTENTS

Dedication

To my wonderful husband who always inspires me to be the best businesswoman I can be. Together, we are winning.

"Leadership is not a person or a position. It is a complex moral relationship between people based on trust, obligation, commitment, emotion, and a shared vision of the good."

– JOANNE CIULLA

Introduction
The Mindset of Success

Success leaves clues. If you study the journeys of accomplished individuals across any field—business, sports, arts, or science—you'll discover a common thread: their mindset. What separates extraordinary achievement from mediocrity isn't just talent or opportunity, but the quality of thoughts that drive actions.

The Power of Your Thoughts

Every day, your mind processes over 60,000 thoughts. These thoughts aren't just fleeting moments of consciousness; they're the architects of your reality. When I share this statistic during my leadership seminars, I often see the same realization dawn across faces: "If my mind is this powerful, why haven't I been more intentional about directing it?"

The answer is simple yet profound—most people never realize they have control over their thought patterns. They experience life reactively, letting circumstances dictate their mental state rather than using their mental state to shape circumstances.

Proverbs 23:7 tells us, *"For as he thinks within himself, so he is."* This ancient wisdom captures a truth modern neuroscience confirms: your thoughts create neural pathways that determine your emotions, actions, and ultimately, your results. You don't just have thoughts—you become them.

The Battleground of Success

Let me ask you a critical question: Where do you believe success and failure are determined?

Many would point to external factors—market conditions, competition, family background, or educational opportunities. While these certainly influence outcomes, they're not the primary battleground.

The real war between success and failure is waged in your mind. Successful people master their thoughts; unsuccessful people are mastered by them.

In my twenty years of business coaching, I've witnessed this truth repeatedly. Two leaders facing identical challenges can experience dramatically different outcomes based solely on their thought patterns. One sees obstacles and retreats; the other sees opportunity and advances. Same situation, different mindset, different results.

Breaking Through Mental Barriers

Consider this story: Two young boys were playing at the edge of their village when the older one, about ten years old, fell into a well. Unable to swim, he began to panic. His friend, just six years old and much smaller, looked around desperately for help.

Finding a rope tied to a bucket, the younger boy threw it into the well and pulled with all his might. His small hands turned red, his feet dug into the ground, but he refused to let go until his friend was safely out.

Later, when they told their parents what happened, no one believed them. How could a skinny six-year-old rescue a robust ten-year-old from a well? The village elders consulted a wise man, who simply said, "It's entirely possible. When the boy helped his friend, there was no one around to tell him he couldn't do it."

This simple story illustrates a profound reality about human potential: the limitations we accept often exist only in our minds. The young boy succeeded because no external voice had planted doubt in his consciousness. His mind was free to accomplish what his heart knew was necessary.

From Mindset to Leadership

As you journey through this book, you'll discover that leadership excellence begins with this same mindset foundation. Before you can lead others effectively, you must first master leading yourself—and that starts with your thoughts.

My own leadership journey began in challenging circumstances. At age eight, I experienced trauma that shaped my perception of trust and relationships. By the time I met my husband in 1992, my mind had constructed a fortress of beliefs about what to expect from others, particularly men. These thought patterns didn't just influence my personal relationships—they affected my ability to lead, delegate, and build genuine connections in business.

It wasn't until I recognized these patterns that I could begin transforming them. The process wasn't easy, but it was necessary. I had to consciously challenge thoughts that whispered limitations:

"Who told you that you couldn't reach your full potential?" "Who told you this is all you deserve?" "Who told you success isn't for people like you?"

These questions became my tools for dismantling mental barriers. And they can become yours as well.

What This Book Offers

"I Am Successful: 5 Keys to Winning in Business" isn't just another leadership manual. It's a roadmap for transforming your mindset to unlock your leadership potential. In the following chapters, you'll discover:

- How to clarify your unique leadership goals and purpose
- Practical communication strategies that inspire and motivate
- Insights for leading across generations, including Millennials and Gen Z
- The 5 Keys framework for sustainable business success
- How to identify and leverage your authentic leadership style
- A clear pathway to leadership readiness and confidence

Each chapter combines practical techniques with mindset principles, creating a comprehensive approach to leadership development. The strategies are concise, actionable, and designed for immediate implementation.

Your Journey Begins Now

As you read these pages, I encourage you to do more than just absorb information. Engage with the ideas actively:

1. Question your existing thought patterns about leadership and success
2. Apply the principles to your current situation, whether

you're leading a corporation, a small team, or preparing for future leadership roles

3. Complete the reflection exercises at the end of each chapter
4. Track your mindset shifts and leadership growth throughout the process

Remember, leadership isn't just about what you do—it's about who you become. And who you become starts with how you think.

John Quincy Adams once said, "If your actions inspire others to dream more, learn more, do more, and become more, you are a leader." This inspiration begins with your mindset. When you transform your thoughts, you transform your leadership, and ultimately, you transform lives—including your own.

Let's begin this transformation together.

Chapter 1
What Are Your Goals as a Leader?

Leadership isn't a position—it's a purpose. Whether you're a CEO, team supervisor, entrepreneur, community organizer, or parent, your effectiveness as a leader depends largely on the clarity of your goals. Without a defined purpose, leadership becomes reactive rather than intentional, responding to immediate demands without building toward a greater vision.

The Purpose Beyond the Position

Many people aspire to leadership positions for various reasons: authority, recognition, compensation, or the opportunity to make decisions. But these external markers of leadership are merely byproducts of the position, not its purpose. True leadership begins with a deeper question: *Why do you want to lead?*

This question invites self-reflection beyond career ambition. As Simon Sinek, author of Start with Why, puts it: "People don't buy what you do; they buy why you do it. And what you do simply proves what you believe."[1] The same principle applies to leadership. People don't follow your title; they follow your purpose. Your leadership "why" becomes the magnetic force that attracts others to your vision.

---

1   Simon Sinek, *Start with Why: How Great Leaders Inspire Everyone to Take Action* (New York: Portfolio, 2009), 41.

Leadership Contexts

Before defining specific leadership goals, it's important to recognize that leadership manifests in multiple contexts:

Organizational Leadership: The formal leadership role within a business or nonprofit structure. This includes executive positions, middle management, and team leadership.

Community Leadership: Guiding initiatives, movements, or programs that serve public interests beyond a single organization.

Thought Leadership: Advancing ideas, innovations, or perspectives that influence how others think about key issues in your field.

Family Leadership: Directing the development, values, and well-being of your household and extended family connections.

Self-Leadership: Managing your own growth, decisions, and personal development as the foundation for leading others.

Your leadership goals may span several of these contexts or focus primarily on one. Recognizing which domains are most relevant to your situation helps clarify appropriate goals.

Five Categories of Leadership Goals

Leadership goals generally fall into five key categories, each representing a different dimension of impact:

1. Performance & Results Goals

These goals focus on measurable outcomes: profit margins, growth metrics, production targets, or other key performance indicators. For many business leaders, performance goals represent the most visible and immediate measure of leadership success.

Jack Welch, former CEO of General Electric, was known for his relentless focus on performance, believing that every business unit should be first or second in its market or be restructured.[2] This clear performance standard guided GE's strategic decisions throughout his tenure.

While performance metrics offer concrete feedback, they represent only one dimension of leadership impact. A leader solely focused on performance metrics may achieve short-term results at the expense of sustainability, innovation, or team development.

Reflection question: What specific, measurable results would demonstrate success in your leadership context?

2. People Development Goals

These goals center on growing the capabilities, confidence, and contributions of those you lead. Great leaders view their role as developing other leaders, not just directing followers.

John C. Maxwell, leadership expert and author, argues that "a leader's lasting value is measured by succession."[3] The true test of leadership isn't what happens when you're present, but what continues when you're gone. People development goals recognize this long-term perspective.

Developing others requires intentional investment: providing challenging assignments, offering meaningful feedback, creating learning opportunities, and gradually releasing authority as capabilities grow.

---

2   Jack Welch and Suzy Welch, *Winning* (New York: HarperBusiness, 2005), 107.
3   John C. Maxwell, *The 21 Irrefutable Laws of Leadership: Follow Them and People Will Follow You* (Nashville: Thomas Nelson, 2007), 227.

Reflection question: How will the people around you be different (more skilled, confident, or empowered) because of your leadership?

3. Vision & Legacy Goals

These goals address the lasting impact you hope to create—the transformation that outlives your direct involvement. Vision goals look beyond immediate results to the horizon of possibility.

Walt Disney's leadership was driven by a vision that extended far beyond entertainment products. "If you can dream it, you can do it," he famously said, establishing a legacy of imagination and innovation that continues to shape the Disney company decades after his death.[4]

Vision goals connect daily decisions to transcendent purpose, giving meaning to mundane tasks and inspiring perseverance through challenges.

Reflection question: What meaningful change do you want your leadership to create that will continue long after your direct involvement ends?

4. Social Impact Goals

These goals focus on how your leadership contributes to broader societal benefit—addressing injustice, solving community problems, or advancing human flourishing beyond your immediate sphere.

Rosalind Brewer, CEO of Walgreens Boots Alliance, defines her leadership purpose partly through social impact: "I want to make sure that in everything I do, I'm bringing other people along...

---

[4]   Pat Williams with Jim Denney, *How to Be Like Walt: Capturing the Disney Magic Every Day of Your Life* (Deerfield Beach, FL: Health Communications, 2004), 57.

especially women and people of color."[5] This social purpose informs her organizational leadership strategies.

In an era where stakeholder capitalism increasingly supplements shareholder capitalism, social impact goals have moved from peripheral to central for many leaders.

Reflection question: How does your leadership address needs or opportunities beyond your organization's boundaries?

5. Personal Growth Goals

These goals focus on your own development as a leader—acquiring new skills, understanding, perspectives, or capacities that enhance your leadership effectiveness.

Warren Bennis, pioneering scholar in leadership studies, observed that "becoming a leader is synonymous with becoming yourself."[6] Personal growth goals recognize leadership as a journey of ongoing development rather than a destination.

The most effective leaders maintain a learning posture throughout their careers, continuously expanding their capacity to navigate complexity and uncertainty.

Reflection question: What personal limitations most constrain your leadership effectiveness currently, and how can you address them?

---

5   Adam Bryant, "Rosalind Brewer of Walgreens on the Power of Really Listening," *New York Times,* October 29, 2021, https://www.nytimes.com/2021/10/29/business/rosalind-brewer-walgreens-corner-office.html.

6   Warren Bennis, *On Becoming a Leader* (New York: Basic Books, 2009), 9.

Finding Your Leadership Purpose

While most leaders have goals across all five categories, effective leadership often stems from clarity about which dimensions matter most to you. Your leadership purpose represents the unique contribution you're positioned to make—your distinctive "why."

To clarify your leadership purpose, consider these questions:

1. Motivation: What initially drew you to leadership, and what sustains your commitment during challenges?

2. Strengths: What capabilities, experiences, or perspectives do you bring that others might not?

3. Passion: What aspects of leadership energize you rather than drain you?

4. Values: What principles are non-negotiable in how you approach leadership?

5. Impact: If your leadership succeeds completely, what specific difference will it make?

These questions help reveal the authentic leadership purpose that aligns with your identity rather than imposing an external leadership template.

SMART Leadership Goals

Once you've clarified your broader leadership purpose, translating it into actionable goals becomes essential. The SMART framework provides a useful structure:

Specific: Precisely what outcome are you pursuing? Vague aspirations like "improve team performance" lack the clarity needed for focused action. A specific goal might be "increase department productivity by

15% while maintaining or improving quality metrics."

Measurable: How will you know if you're making progress? Effective goals include clear metrics for evaluation, whether quantitative (sales figures, engagement scores) or qualitative (client feedback, team development milestones).

Achievable: Is this goal realistic given your resources and constraints? Stretch goals inspire growth, but impossible goals lead to frustration and disengagement.

Relevant: Does this goal align with your broader leadership purpose and organizational needs? Goals disconnected from core priorities diffuse focus and undermine momentum.

Time-bound: What's your timeframe for achievement? Goals without deadlines tend to drift indefinitely, repeatedly postponed by more urgent matters.

Research suggests that formal goal-setting using frameworks like SMART significantly improves leadership outcomes. A study published in the Journal of Leadership & Organizational Studies found that leaders who engaged in structured goal-setting demonstrated 28% higher achievement rates than those with similar aspirations but no formal goal structure.[7]

Balancing Competing Goals

Perhaps the greatest leadership challenge is balancing goals that sometimes appear in tension:

---

7   Timothy A. Judge and Ronald F. Piccolo, "Transformational and Transactional Leadership: A Meta-Analytic Test of Their Relative Validity," *Journal of Applied Psychology* 89, no. 5 (2004): 755-768.

- Short-term results vs. long-term sustainability
- Individual achievement vs. team development
- Organizational needs vs. personal values
- Stability vs. innovation
- Work engagement vs. personal well-being

Effective leadership doesn't require sacrificing one priority for another but rather finding the dynamic balance that serves your unique context and purpose. Jim Collins and Jerry Porras, in their influential book Built to Last, call this embracing the "Genius of the AND" rather than the "Tyranny of the OR"—recognizing that truly great leadership often reconciles apparent contradictions.[8]

Your Leadership Goals Statement

As you conclude this chapter, take time to draft a personal leadership goals statement that captures your primary aims across the five dimensions. This doesn't need to be a polished document, but rather a working compass that guides your leadership decisions and development.

A sample leadership goals statement might read:

"My leadership aims to develop high-performing teams that consistently exceed customer expectations (performance) while growing team members' capabilities and confidence (people development). I'm working to establish innovative approaches to sustainability challenges (vision) that benefit both our organization and the communities we serve (social impact). To achieve these goals, I'm committed to developing greater emotional intelligence and strategic thinking capacity (personal growth)."

---

8   Jim Collins and Jerry I. Porras, *Built to Last: Successful Habits of Visionary Companies* (New York: HarperBusiness, 2004), 43-45.

Your leadership goals statement should reflect your authentic purpose, not an imposed template. Revisit and refine it regularly as your leadership context evolves.

Remember that leadership goals aren't just about what you want to achieve, but who you want to become. As Peter Drucker wisely noted, "The best way to predict the future is to create it."[9] Your leadership goals represent your commitment to creating a future worth pursuing—for yourself, your organization, and those you're privileged to lead.

---

9   Peter F. Drucker, *The Ecological Vision: Reflections on the American Condition* (New York: Routledge, 1993), 122.

Chapter 2
Leaders and Commuication

If leadership is the engine that drives organizational success, communication is the oil that keeps that engine running smoothly. Without effective communication, even the most brilliant vision remains unrealized, the most talented team underperforms, and the most promising strategy fails to launch.

The Communication Gap

Despite its critical importance, communication remains a persistent challenge for many leaders. A study by Interact/Harris Poll revealed a startling statistic: 91% of employees believe their leaders lack effective communication skills.[1] This perception gap between how leaders think they communicate and how their messages are actually received creates friction throughout organizations.

The consequences of poor leadership communication are far-reaching:

- Strategic initiatives stall due to misalignment and confusion
- Employee engagement suffers when expectations are unclear

---

1   Lou Solomon, "The Top Complaints from Employees About Their Leaders," *Harvard Business Review,* June 24, 2015, https://hbr.org/2015/06/the-top-complaints-from-employees-about-their-leaders.

- Innovation slows when ideas aren't effectively shared and developed
- Trust erodes when communication lacks transparency or consistency
- Conflicts escalate when concerns aren't properly addressed

Conversely, organizations with leaders who communicate effectively experience 47% higher returns to shareholders, according to research from Tower Watson.[2] The business case for communication excellence is compelling.

The Communication Framework for Leaders

Effective leadership communication isn't merely about disseminating information—it's about creating shared understanding, building trust, inspiring action, and fostering connection. Let's explore the essential elements of the leadership communication framework:

1. Clarity of Expectations

Nothing frustrates teams more than unclear expectations. When people don't know exactly what success looks like, they waste energy guessing, make preventable mistakes, and ultimately disengage.

Warren Buffett aptly notes, "You can't produce a baby in one month by getting nine women pregnant."[3] His point: clarity about timelines and outcomes prevents misalignment. Similarly, in your leadership communication, specificity matters.

---

2   Tower Watson, "Capitalizing on Effective Communication: How Courage, Innovation and Discipline Drive Business Results in Challenging Times," 2009/2010 Communication ROI Study Report.
3   Warren Buffett, Letter to Shareholders of Berkshire Hathaway, Inc., February 28, 1985.

Practical Application:

- Define what "good" looks like with measurable indicators
- Communicate both the "what" and the "why" behind expectations
- Confirm understanding by asking team members to restate expectations in their own words
- Document important expectations in writing for reference
- Revisit and clarify expectations when circumstances change

2. Active Listening

Communication isn't just about what you say—it's equally about what you hear. Stephen Covey, author of *The 7 Habits of Highly Effective People,* observes: "Most people do not listen with the intent to understand; they listen with the intent to reply."[4]

Active listening—making a conscious effort to understand the complete message being transmitted—transforms leadership effectiveness. When people feel truly heard, trust deepens, insights emerge, and collaboration strengthens.

Practical Application:

- Maintain eye contact and eliminate distractions during conversations
- Ask clarifying questions that probe beneath surface statements

---

4   Stephen R. Covey, *The 7 Habits of Highly Effective People: Powerful Lessons in Personal Change* (New York: Free Press, 2004), 251.

- Paraphrase what you've heard to confirm understanding
- Notice non-verbal cues that might signal unspoken concerns
- Resist the urge to formulate your response while others are still speaking

3. Authentic Presence

In an age of corporate speak and carefully crafted messaging, authenticity stands out. People can detect insincerity, and it undermines their trust in leadership. As organizational psychologist Adam Grant notes, "Being yourself is much easier than pretending to be someone else."[5]

Authentic communication doesn't mean sharing every thought or emotion without filter. Rather, it's about bringing your genuine self to interactions—speaking from personal conviction, acknowledging limitations, and maintaining consistency between your words and actions.

Practical Application:

- Share personal stories that reveal your values and experiences
- Admit when you don't have all the answers
- Express emotions appropriately rather than masking them
- Align your communication style with your natural personality
- Maintain consistency between your public and private messaging

---

5   Adam Grant, *Think Again: The Power of Knowing What You Don't Know* (New York: Viking, 2021), 103.

4. Multi-Channel Messaging

Different people process information differently. Some grasp concepts immediately through verbal explanation; others need visual representation; still others understand best through hands-on experience.

Effective leaders recognize these varied learning styles and adapt their communication accordingly. They employ multiple channels and formats to ensure their message reaches everyone, regardless of preferred learning style.

Practical Application:

- Supplement verbal instructions with visual aids when explaining complex concepts
- Use stories and metaphors to make abstract ideas concrete
- Create opportunities for experiential learning when introducing new processes
- Provide both the big picture and detailed specifications
- Reinforce important messages across multiple mediums (meetings, emails, visuals)

5. Feedback Fluency

The ability to deliver constructive feedback—and receive it graciously—distinguishes exceptional leaders. Without effective feedback, growth stagnates and problems fester.

Kim Scott, author of *Radical Candor,* proposes that effective feedback combines caring personally with challenging directly.[6] When feedback

---

6   Kim Scott, *Radical Candor: Be a Kick-Ass Boss Without Losing Your Humanity* (New York: St. Martin's Press, 2017), 25-27.

comes from a place of genuine concern for someone's development, even difficult messages can be received positively.

Practical Application:

- Deliver timely feedback rather than saving it for formal reviews
- Focus feedback on specific behaviors rather than character
- Balance constructive criticism with genuine appreciation
- Ask permission before offering unsolicited feedback
- Model receptivity by actively seeking feedback on your own performance

6. Crisis Communication

A leader's communication ability faces its ultimate test during crises. Whether managing an organizational restructuring, responding to market disruption, or navigating a global pandemic, crisis situations demand heightened communication skill.

James Haggerty, crisis management expert, notes that "in the absence of communication, negative speculation fills the void."[7] Leaders who communicate transparently and frequently during crises maintain trust and morale even through difficult circumstances.

Practical Application:

- Communicate early and often, even when information is incomplete

---

7   James F. Haggerty, *Chief Crisis Officer: Structure and Leadership for Effective Communications Response* (Chicago: ABA Publishing, 2017), 83.

- Acknowledge what you know, what you don't know, and what you're doing to learn more
- Address emotional concerns before tactical details
- Maintain consistency across all spokespersons
- Follow up regularly as the situation evolves

Digital Communication for Leaders

Today's leaders must navigate an increasingly digital communication landscape. Remote work, global teams, and digital collaboration tools have transformed how leaders connect with their people.

While digital communication offers unprecedented reach and efficiency, it also presents unique challenges. Research from Harvard Business Review found that digital messages are more likely to be misinterpreted than face-to-face communication, with recipients rating the same message as 50% more negative when received digitally versus in person.[8]

Digital Communication Best Practices:
- Choose the right medium for the message. Complex, sensitive, or emotionally charged topics usually warrant synchronous communication (video call or phone) rather than asynchronous methods (email or messaging).
- Establish clear digital communication norms. Set expectations about response times, appropriate channels for different types of communication, and when to take conversations offline.

---

8   Justin Kruger and Nicholas Epley, "When What You Type Isn't What They Read: The Perseverance of Stereotypes and Expectancies Over E-mail," *Journal of Experimental Social Psychology* 41, no. 4 (2005): 414-422.

- Compensate for missing non-verbal cues. In text-based communication, be more explicit about tone and intent than you would in person. Consider using emojis or explicit emotional labeling when appropriate.
- Create intentional connection moments. Digital environments can feel isolating. Schedule regular check-ins focused on relationship-building, not just task updates.
- Practice digital empathy. Remember that digital communication exists in a broader context of each person's life circumstances. Extend grace for miscommunications and technical challenges.

The Storytelling Leader

Throughout human history, stories have been our most powerful communication tool. Our brains are literally wired for narrative—we process, remember, and connect through stories in ways that data and directives alone cannot achieve.

Neuroscientist Paul Zak found that character-driven stories consistently cause the brain to produce oxytocin, a neurochemical that enhances empathy and motivates cooperation.[9] For leaders, storytelling isn't just engaging—it's neurologically effective.

Leadership Storytelling Applications:

- Vision stories that illustrate what success will look like when achieved

---

9   Paul J. Zak, "Why Your Brain Loves Good Storytelling," *Harvard Business Review*, October 28, 2014, https://hbr.org/2014/10/why-your-brain-loves-good-storytelling.

- Origin stories that convey organizational values through founding moments
- Challenge stories that build resilience by recounting obstacles overcome
- Customer stories that connect daily work to real-world impact
- Failure stories that normalize learning and create psychological safety
- Personal stories that reveal vulnerability and build authentic connection

The Communication Development Plan

Like any leadership skill, communication improves with intentional practice and feedback. Consider these steps to enhance your leadership communication:

1. Assess your current communication effectiveness. Solicit honest feedback from peers, direct reports, and supervisors about your communication strengths and opportunities.
2. Identify your primary development area. Rather than trying to improve everything at once, focus on the one or two aspects of communication that would most enhance your leadership impact.
3. Seek exemplars and resources. Find leaders who excel in your focus area and observe their techniques. Consider books, courses, or coaching to accelerate your development.
4. Create practice opportunities. Deliberately put yourself in situations that require your target communication skill, perhaps starting in lower-stakes environments.

5. Request ongoing feedback. Ask trusted colleagues to observe specific aspects of your communication and provide constructive input.
6. Reflect and adjust. Regularly assess your progress and refine your approach based on what's working and what isn't.

Communication as Connection

At its core, leadership communication isn't just about transmitting information—it's about creating connection. When we communicate effectively, we bridge the gap between separate individuals to create shared understanding, purpose, and commitment.

Maya Angelou wisely observed, "People will forget what you said, people will forget what you did, but people will never forget how you made them feel."[10] This truth lies at the heart of leadership communication. Beyond the words and tactics, effective communicators make others feel valued, understood, inspired, and empowered.

As you develop your leadership communication skills, remember that the goal isn't perfection but connection. When you approach communication as a means of genuine human connection rather than mere information transfer, your leadership influence naturally expands.

---

10   Maya Angelou, interview by Dave Chappelle, *The Sundance Channel,* February 22, 2006.

Chapter 3
Leadership and Millennials & Gen Z

The workplace landscape has transformed dramatically over the past decade. Traditional leadership approaches that worked for previous generations often fall flat with today's workforce dominated by Millennials and the rising presence of Generation Z. Understanding these generational shifts isn't just helpful—it's essential for leadership effectiveness in the contemporary business world.

The Generational Landscape

For the first time in history, four distinct generations work side by side in many organizations:

- Baby Boomers (born 1946-1964), though increasingly retiring
- Generation X (born 1965-1980)
- Millennials (born 1981-1996)
- Generation Z (born 1997-2012)

According to the Bureau of Labor Statistics, Millennials became the largest generation in the U.S. workforce in 2016, comprising nearly 35% of all workers.[1] Meanwhile, Generation Z is entering

---

1   Richard Fry, "Millennials are the Largest Generation in the U.S. Labor Force," *Pew Research Center,* April 11, 2018, https://www.pewresearch.org/fact-tank/2018/04/11/millennials-largest-generation-us-labor-force/.

the workforce at an accelerating rate, projected to constitute 30% of employees by 2030.[2]

Rather than perpetuating generational stereotypes, effective leaders recognize both the commonalities and distinct characteristics that shape generational workplace preferences and motivations.

Understanding Millennial Leadership Expectations

Millennials grew up during rapid technological change, economic uncertainty, and increased globalization. These experiences shaped distinctive workplace expectations that affect how they respond to leadership.

1. Purpose-Driven Work

Unlike previous generations that might have prioritized stability or advancement, Millennials seek meaning and purpose in their work. A Deloitte survey found that 86% of Millennials believe business success should be measured by more than just financial performance.[3]

Leadership Implication: Connect organizational goals to broader impact. Clearly articulate how daily work contributes to meaningful outcomes that extend beyond profit margins. As one Harvard Business Review study noted, "Millennials view work as a key part of life, not a separate activity that needs to be balanced by it."[4]

---

2   Josh Bersin and Tomas Chamorro-Premuzic, "The Case for Hiring Older Workers," *Harvard Business Review,* September 26, 2019, https://hbr.org/2019/09/the-case-for-hiring-older-workers.

3   Deloitte, "The Deloitte Global Millennial Survey 2020," 2020, https://www2.deloitte.com/global/en/pages/about-deloitte/articles/millennialsurvey.html.

4   Jeanne C. Meister and Karie Willyerd, "Mentoring Millennials," *Harvard Business Review,* May 2010, https://hbr.org/2010/05/mentoring-millennials.

2. Flexibility and Autonomy

The traditional 9-to-5 office model appears increasingly antiquated to a generation raised with digital connectivity. Even before the pandemic accelerated remote work adoption, YPulse research found that 68% of 18-34-year-olds believed they would enjoy a job more if it allowed working remotely.[5]

Leadership Implication: Focus on results rather than process whenever possible. Create flexible work arrangements that emphasize outcomes over hours logged. Trust employees to manage their time and location while holding them accountable for deliverables.

3. Continuous Feedback and Growth

The annual performance review cycle feels painfully outdated to Millennials accustomed to immediate feedback in digital environments. Research by SuccessFactors and Oxford Economics revealed that 75% of Millennials want more frequent feedback from their managers.[6]

Leadership Implication: Implement regular check-ins and real-time feedback. Create development plans that address both immediate skill needs and long-term career aspirations. As Bill Gates observed, "We all need people who will give us feedback. That's how we improve."[7]

4. Collaborative Leadership

Hierarchical, command-and-control leadership models often

---

5   YPulse, "Millennials Wanted to Work From Home, This Isn't What They Meant," May 7, 2020, https://www.ypulse.com/article/2020/05/07/millennials-wanted-to-work-from-home-this-isnt-what-they-meant/.
6   SuccessFactors and Oxford Economics, "Millennials at Work," 2014.
7   Bill Gates, quoted in Alan Murray, "America's Top CEOs Talk Leadership," *Wall Street Journal*, October 23, 2010.

alienate Millennials who expect to contribute ideas regardless of their position in the organizational chart. They were raised in educational environments that emphasized group projects and collaborative problem-solving.

Leadership Implication: Create opportunities for input and co-creation. Build decision-making processes that incorporate diverse perspectives while maintaining clarity about final accountability. As leadership expert John C. Maxwell notes, "The leader who thinks he's leading but has no one following him is only taking a walk."[8]

The Rise of Generation Z

While Millennials have received extensive attention, Generation Z is rapidly entering the workforce with their own distinct characteristics. Born roughly between 1997 and 2012, these digital natives have never known a world without smartphones and social media. Early research indicates several key differences from their Millennial predecessors:

1. Digital Fluency with Offline Balance

Unlike Millennials who adapted to digital technology, Gen Z was born into it. They move seamlessly between digital and physical environments but are increasingly aware of digital burnout. According to a study by Deloitte and Network of Executive Women, 37% of Gen Z reports putting their phone away to focus on tasks, compared to just 24% of Millennials.[9]

---

8   John C. Maxwell, *The 21 Irrefutable Laws of Leadership: Follow Them and People Will Follow You* (Nashville: Thomas Nelson, 2007), 51.
9   Deloitte and Network of Executive Women, "Welcome to Generation Z," 2019, https://www2.deloitte.com/us/en/pages/consumer-business/articles/understanding-generation-z-consumer.html.

Leadership Implication: Leverage their digital capabilities while creating boundaries that prevent burnout. Design workflows that integrate technology meaningfully rather than for its own sake. Provide opportunities for face-to-face connection to balance digital communication.

2. Pragmatic Financial Mindset

Having witnessed the Great Recession during formative years and entered adulthood during the economic uncertainty of the pandemic, Gen Z tends to be more financially conservative than Millennials. A study by Bank of America found that 80% of Gen Z is already saving money, and financial security ranks as a top priority.[10]

Leadership Implication: Be transparent about compensation structures and growth opportunities. Communicate clearly how performance connects to financial rewards. Consider offering financial wellness resources as part of your benefits package.

3. Entrepreneurial Orientation

Gen Z shows strong entrepreneurial tendencies, with 41% planning to start their own businesses, according to one Gallup poll.[11] Even within traditional employment, they seek opportunities to innovate and create value independently.

Leadership Implication: Create "intrapreneurial" opportunities within your organization. Assign ownership of projects and initiatives that allow for creative problem-solving and visible impact. Recognize and reward innovation, not just execution.

---

10   Bank of America, "Better Money Habits Millennial Report," Winter 2020.

11   Gallup, "How Millennials Want to Work and Live," 2016.

4. Diversity as Expectation

As the most diverse generation in American history, Gen Z views inclusion not as a corporate initiative but as a baseline expectation. According to research by McKinsey, 76% of Gen Z consumers have discontinued relationships with companies that treated employees, communities, or the environment poorly.[12]

Leadership Implication: Ensure your organization's commitment to diversity and inclusion is authentic and embedded in operations, not just marketing. Create space for difficult conversations about equity and belonging. As management professor Brené Brown notes, "We have to be willing to have the hard conversations."[13]

Bridging the Leadership Gap

Given these generational differences, how can leaders effectively engage across age groups without creating silos or playing favorites? Consider these strategies:

1. Lead with Principles, Not Stereotypes

While generational insights provide useful context, effective leaders recognize individual differences within any age group. Leadership consultant Simon Sinek cautions, "The danger of these generational labels is that they're used for marketing and they make us forget that every single one of us is a human being."[14]

---

12   McKinsey & Company, "Generation Z and Its Implications for Companies," November 12, 2018.
13   Brené Brown, *Dare to Lead: Brave Work. Tough Conversations. Whole Hearts.* (New York: Random House, 2018), 43.
14   Simon Sinek, interview by Inside Quest, "Millennials in the Workplace," October 2016.

Rather than applying generational assumptions, focus on fundamental human needs that transcend age: respect, purpose, growth, connection, and contribution.

2. Create Cross-Generational Mentoring

Traditional mentoring paired senior employees with juniors, but bidirectional mentoring recognizes that knowledge flows both ways. Younger employees offer digital fluency and fresh perspectives, while experienced staff provide institutional knowledge and professional wisdom.

Procter & Gamble implemented a "reverse mentoring" program where Millennial employees coached executives on digital trends and social media, resulting in improved strategic decisions and stronger intergenerational relationships.[15]

3. Flex Your Communication Style

Different generations often have distinct communication preferences:

- Baby Boomers may prefer face-to-face meetings and phone calls
- Gen X might favor email and structured meetings
- Millennials typically embrace texting, collaboration platforms, and video calls
- Gen Z often prefers brief visual communication and instant messaging

Effective leaders adjust their communication approach based on audience needs while gradually moving toward shared organizational norms.

---

15   Hari Abburi, "The Surprising Truth About What Millennials Really Want at Work," *ERE,* September 19, 2018, https://www.ere.net/the-surprising-truth-about-what-millennials-really-want-at-work/.

4. Focus on Results, Not Methods

Rather than mandating how work gets done, define clear outcomes and give teams flexibility in execution. This approach respects generational differences in work style while maintaining performance standards.

Microsoft CEO Satya Nadella embodies this approach: "Don't be a know-it-all; be a learn-it-all."[16] This mindset creates space for multiple approaches to solving problems, regardless of age or experience level.

Leading Through Generational Transitions

As Baby Boomers retire and Generation Alpha (born after 2012) begins entering the workforce in the coming years, generational transitions will remain a constant leadership challenge. Organizations that thrive during these shifts share several characteristics:

1. Clear values that transcend generations
2. Continuous adaptation of policies and practices
3. Regular feedback loops with employees of all ages
4. Genuine appreciation for diverse perspectives
5. Focus on human connection amid technological change

Final Thoughts: Beyond Generational Differences

While understanding generational characteristics provides valuable context, exceptional leaders recognize the limitations of generational generalizations. Cultural background, individual personality,

---

16   Satya Nadella, *Hit Refresh: The Quest to Rediscover Microsoft's Soul and Imagine a Better Future for Everyone* (New York: HarperBusiness, 2017), 76.

professional experience, and life circumstances often influence workplace behavior more profoundly than birth year.

As management thinker Peter Drucker observed long before the term "Millennial" entered our vocabulary: "The best way to predict the future is to create it."[17] The future of multi-generational leadership depends not on categorizing differences but on creating environments where human potential thrives regardless of when someone was born.

The most effective approach combines generational awareness with individual attention. Take time to understand the unique history, motivations, and aspirations of each person you lead. Listen to their stories, observe their work preferences, and adjust your leadership approach accordingly.

In doing so, you'll discover that while generational insights provide useful context, leadership excellence ultimately transcends age, connecting with the fundamental human needs and aspirations we all share.

---

17   Peter F. Drucker, *The Ecological Vision: Reflections on the American Condition* (New York: Routledge, 1993), 122.

Chapter 4
The 5 Keys to Winning in Business

Success in business rarely happens by accident. While luck occasionally plays a role, sustainable achievement comes from intentional practices that build momentum over time. After studying successful leaders and organizations—and through my own experience developing leaders—I've identified five fundamental keys that consistently unlock business success.

These keys aren't just theoretical concepts; they're practical principles you can implement immediately. They work regardless of your industry, the size of your organization, or your leadership experience. When applied consistently, they create the conditions for both business growth and personal fulfillment.

The 5 Keys Framework

Before diving into each key individually, it's important to understand how they work together as an integrated system:

- Key 1: Create the Culture establishes the foundation
- Key 2: Choose Your Circle determines your support system
- Key 3: Cultivate Integrity builds your leadership character
- Key 4: Focus on Growth drives continuous improvement
- Key 5: Add Value Through Delegation multiplies your impact

While each key delivers value independently, their power compounds when implemented together. Let's explore each key in depth.

Key 1: Create the Culture—Make People Feel Appreciated

"Culture eats strategy for breakfast," management guru Peter Drucker famously observed.[1] No matter how brilliant your business plan, the environment you create ultimately determines your success.

Culture isn't just a corporate buzzword—it's the invisible force shaping behavior, decisions, and results throughout your organization. As a leader, you don't just participate in culture; you establish it. Every interaction, decision, and priority you set communicates what truly matters.

The Science of Appreciation

Research consistently demonstrates that feeling valued is a fundamental human need. A landmark study published in the Journal of Personality and Social Psychology found that the brain processes social rewards (like recognition) through the same neural pathways as monetary rewards.[22] In other words, appreciation activates the brain's reward center just as powerfully as financial incentives.

Organizations that establish appreciation-rich cultures enjoy concrete benefits:

---

1   This quote is often attributed to Peter Drucker, though there is debate about whether he actually said it. The concept was popularized by Mark Fields, former president of Ford.

2   Tamir, Diana I., and Jason P. Mitchell. "Disclosing Information About the Self Is Intrinsically Rewarding." *Proceedings of the National Academy of Sciences* 109, no. 21 (2012): 8038-8043.

- 31% lower voluntary turnover[3]
- 21% higher profitability[4]
- 41% reduction in quality defects and safety incidents[5]

Creating a Culture of Appreciation

Culture forms through both intentional design and unconscious modeling. Consider these strategies for building appreciation into your cultural DNA:

Make recognition specific and timely. Generic praise has minimal impact. Instead, acknowledge specific contributions immediately after they occur. For example, rather than saying "Good job on that project," try "The market research you included in your presentation helped us make a much better decision."

Align recognition with values. When you recognize behaviors that exemplify your core values, you reinforce what matters most. This creates a virtuous cycle where people naturally gravitate toward value-aligned actions.

Diversify your appreciation approaches. People respond differently to various forms of recognition. Some prefer public acknowledgment, while others value private conversations. Some appreciate verbal praise, while others prefer written notes. A study by Gallup found that the most effective recognition is honest, authentic, and individualized.[6]

---

3   Gallup, "State of the American Workplace," 2017
4   Jessica Rohman, "Building a Recognition Culture: The ROI of Recognition," *Great Place to Work,* 2019.
5   Alexander Kjerulf, *Happy Hour is 9 to 5* (Copenhagen: Pine Tribe, 2014), 124.
6   Gallup, "Employee Recognition: Low Cost, High Impact," June 28, 2016.

Create systems for peer recognition. While leadership appreciation matters enormously, peer recognition often carries special significance. Implement platforms or practices that enable team members to acknowledge each other's contributions.

Measure cultural health. What gets measured gets managed. Regularly assess your culture through surveys, focus groups, and observation. Pay particular attention to whether people feel valued for their contributions.

Remember, culture isn't created through grand announcements or value statements on the wall—it's built through consistent, everyday actions that communicate what truly matters. As leadership expert Jon Gordon notes, "We replicate after our own kind."[7] The appreciation you demonstrate becomes the standard others follow.

Key 2: Choose Your Circle—Recognize Their Unique Qualities

Jim Rohn's famous observation that "you are the average of the five people you spend the most time with" applies not just to personal development but to business success as well.[8] The people surrounding you—your leadership team, advisors, mentors, and close colleagues—profoundly shape your thinking, decisions, and ultimately your results.

Successful leaders intentionally cultivate relationships that elevate rather than diminish their potential. They understand that not everyone deserves equal access to their time and influence.

---

7 Jon Gordon, *The Power of a Positive Team: Proven Principles and Practices That Make Great Teams Great* (Hoboken: Wiley, 2018), 37.
8 Jim Rohn, quoted in Darren Hardy, *The Compound Effect* (New York: Vanguard Press, 2010), 35.

Value-Adding vs. Value-Draining Relationships

Every relationship either adds to or subtracts from your leadership effectiveness. Value-adding relationships energize, challenge, and support you. Value-draining relationships deplete your resources without contributing meaningful returns.

The four essential qualities to seek in those closest to you include:

1. Good Habits

Behavioral science confirms that habits are contagious through social influence.[9] When those around you demonstrate discipline, positivity, and purposeful action, you naturally adopt similar patterns. Conversely, negative habits like chronic complaining, procrastination, or ethical shortcuts can subtly infiltrate your own behavior.

Seek relationships with those who:

- Demonstrate consistent follow-through
- Maintain healthy boundaries
- Practice disciplined decision-making
- Balance work with sustainable self-care

2. Positive Mental Outlook

Stanford psychologist Carol Dweck's research on mindset reveals that our beliefs about potential and challenge significantly impact outcomes.[10] Those with a growth mindset see challenges as

---

9   Nicholas A. Christakis and James H. Fowler, "Social Contagion Theory: Examining Dynamic Social Networks and Human Behavior," *Statistics in Medicine* 32, no. 4 (2013): 556-577.

10   Carol S. Dweck, *Mindset: The New Psychology of Success* (New York: Random House, 2006), 6-7.

opportunities and believe abilities can be developed. Those with a fixed mindset view challenges as threats and believe abilities are static.

Surround yourself with people who:

- Focus on possibilities rather than limitations
- View setbacks as temporary and instructive
- Take responsibility rather than blame circumstances
- Approach challenges with curiosity rather than fear

3. Trustworthiness

Business moves at the speed of trust. When you must constantly verify, double-check, or compensate for others' unreliability, progress slows dramatically. Conversely, high-trust relationships enable efficient decision-making and execution.

Prioritize relationships with those who:

- Maintain confidentiality when appropriate
- Deliver on commitments consistently
- Speak truthfully even when it's difficult
- Place team success above personal gain

4. Fanatic Loyalty

True loyalty goes beyond just showing up. It means actively advancing shared interests, providing honest feedback when needed, and standing firm during difficulties. As Warren Buffett noted, "It takes 20 years to build a reputation and five minutes to ruin it."[11]

---

11   Warren Buffett, interview by Liz Claman, *Fox Business Network,* May 7, 2008.

Value those who demonstrate:

- Commitment to shared long-term vision
- Willingness to have difficult conversations when necessary
- Public support with private feedback
- Consistency during both success and setbacks

Building Your Circle Strategically

Creating a high-value circle doesn't happen accidentally. It requires intentional assessment, development, and sometimes difficult decisions.

<u>Assess your current circle</u>. Evaluate your closest professional relationships against the four qualities above. Which relationships strengthen your leadership? Which drain your effectiveness?

<u>Develop existing relationships</u>. Sometimes the issue isn't the relationship itself but its current state. Consider how to strengthen valuable relationships through better communication, clearer expectations, or renewed commitment.

<u>Expand strategically</u>. Identify gaps in your current circle and seek relationships that provide missing perspectives or capabilities. This might include finding a mentor, joining a mastermind group, or building connections with leaders in adjacent fields.

<u>Make necessary transitions</u>. Some relationships may ultimately prove incompatible with your leadership goals. While severing ties should never be your first approach, sometimes creating distance is necessary for your continued growth.

Key 3: Cultivate Integrity and Character

In a business landscape filled with technical capabilities, strategic positioning, and market forces, character might seem like an abstract concern. Yet integrity remains the foundation upon which all sustainable success is built. As former Medtronic CEO Bill George observes, "If you don't have integrity, you have nothing. You can't buy it. You can have all the money in the world, but if you are not a moral and ethical person, you really have nothing."[12]

The Business Case for Integrity

Beyond moral arguments, integrity delivers tangible business benefits:

Trust acceleration. Organizations led with integrity establish trust more quickly with customers, partners, and employees. This trust translates directly to faster sales cycles, more favorable terms, and greater employee engagement.

Crisis resilience. When challenges inevitably arise, leaders with established reputations for integrity receive greater benefit of the doubt. As Warren Buffett advised, "It takes 20 years to build a reputation and five minutes to ruin it. If you think about that, you'll do things differently."[13]

Talent attraction and retention. Research consistently shows that ethical leadership significantly impacts employee satisfaction and commitment. A study in the Journal of Business Ethics found that

---

12   Bill George, *Authentic Leadership: Rediscovering the Secrets to Creating Lasting Value* (San Francisco: Jossey-Bass, 2003), 18.
13   Warren Buffett, *Letter to Shareholders of Berkshire Hathaway, Inc.,* February 28, 1991.

perceived leader integrity was the strongest predictor of employee job satisfaction across industries.[14]

Living Integrity Daily

Integrity isn't an occasional choice but a consistent pattern of alignment between words and actions. Here are practical ways to strengthen this foundation:

Honor your commitments. Mean what you say and say what you mean. When circumstances change and you cannot fulfill a commitment, communicate proactively rather than making excuses afterward.

Apply consistent standards. Ensure your ethical expectations apply equally to everyone, including yourself. Nothing undermines organizational integrity faster than perceived double standards.

Create accountability structures. Even leaders with the best intentions benefit from accountability. Build relationships and systems that help you maintain your commitments to ethical behavior.

Practice transparent communication. Share information openly except when there are legitimate reasons for confidentiality. When you cannot disclose something, explain why rather than avoiding the topic.

As Martin Luther King Jr. noted, "The time is always right to do what is right."[15] In leadership, integrity isn't just about avoiding

---

14   Michael E. Brown, Linda K. Treviño, and David A. Harrison, "Ethical Leadership: A Social Learning Perspective for Construct Development and Testing," *Organizational Behavior and Human Decision Processes* 97, no. 2 (2005): 117-134.

15   Martin Luther King Jr., "The Future of Integration," speech at Manchester College, February 1, 1968.

wrong actions—it's about proactively choosing right ones, especially when doing so involves personal cost.

Key 4: Focus on Growth—Embrace Humility as an Asset

The leadership graveyard is filled with once-successful executives who stopped growing. In today's environment of accelerating change, leadership development isn't optional—it's survival.

Paradoxically, the foundation for growth isn't confidence but humility—the honest recognition of both your strengths and limitations. Research published in the Journal of Management found that humble leaders had teams with higher performance, greater collaboration, and lower turnover than their more egocentric counterparts.[16]

The Learning Leader Mindset

Effective leaders maintain an active learning orientation throughout their careers. Dr. Carol Dweck's groundbreaking research on mindset reveals that leaders who believe abilities can be developed (growth mindset) consistently outperform those who view talents as fixed.[17]

Cultivate your growth mindset by:

Embracing challenges as growth opportunities. When faced with

---

16   Bradley P. Owens and David R. Hekman, "How Does Leader Humility Influence Team Performance? Exploring the Mechanisms of Contagion and Collective Promotion Focus," *Academy of Management Journal* 59, no. 3 (2016): 1088-1111.
17   Carol S. Dweck, *Mindset: The New Psychology of Success* (New York: Random House, 2006), 108-112.

difficult situations, ask "What can I learn from this?" rather than "How can I get through this?"

Seeking feedback consistently. Create regular opportunities for honest input from diverse sources. The most valuable feedback often comes from unexpected places.

Finding mentors and coaches. Even experienced leaders benefit from outside perspective. Identify people who can see your blind spots and hold you accountable to your growth goals.

Allocating time for reflection. Growth doesn't come from experience alone but from reflecting on experience. Schedule regular intervals to review lessons learned and adjust your approach.

Remember, humility isn't weakness—it's honest self-assessment that creates space for improvement. As C.S. Lewis observed, "Humility is not thinking less of yourself, it's thinking of yourself less."[18]

Key 5: Add Value—Master the Art of Delegation

Your ultimate success isn't measured by what you personally accomplish but by what you enable others to achieve. Effective delegation multiplies your impact exponentially while developing your team's capabilities.

Yet delegation remains one of the most challenging leadership skills to master. A Harvard Business Review study found that 46% of companies were concerned about delegation skills among their leaders.[19]

---

18   C.S. Lewis, *Mere Christianity* (New York: HarperOne, 2001), 128.

19   Jenny Chatman and Lindred Greer, "Why Your Company Needs A Chief Delegation Officer," *Harvard Business Review,* April 13, 2016.

The Delegation Paradox

Many leaders intellectually understand delegation's importance but emotionally resist it. This resistance often stems from:

- Fear that others won't meet your standards
- Concern about losing control of outcomes
- Belief that explaining tasks takes longer than doing them
- Identity attachment to being the primary doer

These concerns reflect a fundamental misunderstanding of delegation's purpose. True delegation isn't about assigning tasks; it's about developing people while achieving results.

Effective Delegation Practices

Transform your approach to delegation with these practices:

Delegate outcomes, not just tasks. Clarify the desired result while giving people flexibility in how they achieve it. This approach encourages innovation and ownership.

Match assignments to development needs. Consider not just current capabilities but growth potential when delegating. The right stretch assignment can accelerate someone's development dramatically.

Provide context, not just content. Help people understand why an assignment matters and how it connects to broader objectives. Context creates meaning that motivates discretionary effort.

Establish clear parameters. Define resources available, decision-making authority, communication expectations, and deadlines. These boundaries create freedom to execute without constant checking.

Support without taking over. When challenges arise, resist the urge to reclaim the assignment. Instead, provide coaching that builds capacity to overcome similar obstacles in the future.

As Richard Branson wisely noted, "Delegation is one of the most important leadership skills. Without the ability to delegate successfully, it would be impossible to effectively expand your business or enterprise."[20]

The 5 Keys in Action

While each key delivers value independently, their power compounds when implemented together. Consider how they reinforce each other:

- A culture of appreciation (Key 1) attracts and retains the high-quality circle you need (Key 2)
- Your integrity (Key 3) establishes the trust necessary for effective delegation (Key 5)
- Humility (Key 4) opens you to learning from your circle (Key 2)
- Proper delegation (Key 5) creates space for continued growth (Key 4)

Start by assessing your current strengths and opportunities across all five keys. Then prioritize one or two areas for immediate focus. Remember that small, consistent improvements compound over time.

Leadership isn't just about what you achieve but who you become in the process. These five keys develop not just your business results but your leadership character—creating success that sustains and fulfills rather than depletes.

---

20   Richard Branson, "Richard Branson on the Art of Delegation," *Entrepreneur*, October 31, 2012.

Chapter 5
What's Your Leadership Style?

Leaders come in all varieties. The assertive visionary who boldly charts new territory. The thoughtful strategist who carefully analyzes every option. The empathetic coach who brings out the best in others. The disciplined executor who ensures consistent results.

No single leadership style works in every situation or for every person. Your most effective approach will align with both your authentic self and the specific needs of those you lead. Understanding different leadership styles—including your natural tendencies—creates the flexibility to adapt your approach as circumstances require.

The Evolution of Leadership Theory

Our understanding of leadership has evolved dramatically over the past century. Early "Great Man" theories suggested leaders were born, not made, possessing inherent traits that destined them for command. By the mid-20th century, behavioral theories shifted focus to what leaders do rather than who they inherently are.

In 1939, psychologist Kurt Lewin and his colleagues conducted groundbreaking research that identified three basic leadership styles: authoritarian, democratic, and laissez-faire.[1] This foundational study

---

1   Kurt Lewin, Ronald Lippitt, and Ralph K. White, "Patterns of Aggressive Behavior in Experimentally Created 'Social Climates,'" *The Journal of Social Psychology* 10, no. 2 (1939): 269-299.

revealed that different approaches produced distinctly different outcomes in group dynamics, performance, and satisfaction.

Since then, leadership theory has expanded to recognize a broader spectrum of styles, each with its own strengths and limitations. Let's explore the major leadership approaches to help you identify your natural tendencies and develop greater stylistic versatility.

The Leadership Style Spectrum

1. Authoritarian (Autocratic) Leadership

Core approach: Leaders make decisions unilaterally with little input from team members.

When it works best:

- Crisis situations requiring immediate decisions
- Environments with inexperienced team members needing clear direction
- Contexts where consistency and standardization are critical
- Situations with significant safety or compliance requirements

Limitations:

- Reduces team creativity and initiative
- Creates dependence on the leader
- Increases stress and reduces job satisfaction
- May create resistance or compliance without commitment

Military leaders often employ this style effectively. General George S. Patton exemplified authoritarian leadership during World War II, making quick, decisive commands that left little room for debate.[2] While controversial, his approach proved effective during wartime conditions requiring immediate action.

2. Democratic (Participative) Leadership

Core approach: Leaders involve team members in decision-making while maintaining final authority.

When it works best:

- Complex problems requiring diverse perspectives
- Teams with specialized expertise the leader lacks
- Situations where buy-in is essential for implementation
- Environments focused on innovation and creativity

Limitations:

- Decision-making can be slower
- May create frustration when urgent action is needed
- Can appear indecisive if overused
- Requires skilled facilitation to be effective

Former President Dwight D. Eisenhower exemplified democratic leadership during the planning of the D-Day invasion, famously saying: "Leadership is the art of getting someone else to do something you want done because he wants to do it."[3] He skillfully incorporated input from diverse military leaders while maintaining clear decision authority.

---

2   Carlo D'Este, *Patton: A Genius for War* (New York: HarperCollins, 1995), 536-538.

3   Dwight D. Eisenhower, speech to National Defense Executive Reserve Conference, November 14, 1956.

3. Laissez-faire (Delegative) Leadership

Core approach: Leaders provide resources and support but give substantial autonomy to team members.

When it works best:

- Highly skilled, self-motivated teams
- Creative or research-oriented work
- Environments where innovation is prioritized over standardization
- Development opportunities for future leaders

Limitations:

- Can create confusion about priorities
- May result in lack of coordination between team members
- Often leads to missed deadlines without appropriate structure
- Can be perceived as disinterest or abandonment

Google's "20% time" policy, which allowed engineers to spend one-fifth of their work time on self-directed projects, represents a structured form of laissez-faire leadership.[4] This approach produced innovations like Gmail and Google News, demonstrating the creative potential of appropriate autonomy.

4. Servant Leadership

Core approach: Leaders focus primarily on serving the needs of their team members, removing obstacles to their success.

---

4   Eric Schmidt and Jonathan Rosenberg, *How Google Works* (New York: Grand Central Publishing, 2014), 134-135.

When it works best:

- Environments valuing long-term employee development
- Organizations with strong mission orientation
- Contexts requiring deep employee commitment
- Teams needing healing after toxic leadership experiences

Limitations:

- May struggle with necessary but unpopular decisions
- Can sometimes lack necessary assertiveness
- Might create slower response in crisis situations
- Requires genuine commitment to appear authentic

Cheryl Bachelder, former CEO of Popeyes Louisiana Kitchen, demonstrated servant leadership by focusing intently on supporting franchise owners' success. During her tenure, profitability soared as she prioritized serving those closest to customers.[5] Her approach transformed both culture and financial results.

5. Transformational Leadership

Core approach: Leaders inspire and stimulate followers to achieve extraordinary outcomes while developing their own leadership capacity.

When it works best:

- Organizations needing significant change
- Environments where innovation is essential
- Teams that have become complacent
- Contexts requiring deep engagement and commitment

---

5   Cheryl Bachelder, *Dare to Serve: How to Drive Superior Results by Serving Others* (Oakland: Berrett-Koehler Publishers, 2015), 27-31.

Limitations:

- Can create unrealistic expectations
- May burn out both leaders and followers
- Sometimes prioritizes vision over practical execution
- Requires strong communication skills to be effective

Steve Jobs exemplified transformational leadership at Apple, challenging employees to "put a dent in the universe" while driving relentless innovation.[6] His compelling vision pulled people beyond incremental improvements toward revolutionary products, despite his sometimes difficult interpersonal approach.

6. Transactional Leadership

Core approach: Leaders establish clear structures with explicit rewards and consequences linked to performance.

When it works best:

- Environments with clear, measurable objectives
- Crisis situations requiring immediate performance improvement
- Contexts with significant compliance requirements
- Teams needing clear direction and accountability

Limitations:

- Often generates compliance rather than commitment
- May reduce intrinsic motivation over time
- Typically maintains rather than transforms
- Can create transitory rather than sustainable results

---

6   Walter Isaacson, *Steve Jobs* (New York: Simon & Schuster, 2011), 570-571.

Alan Mulally's leadership at Ford Motor Company during its turnaround demonstrated effective transactional elements.[7] His data-driven weekly Business Plan Review meetings created clear accountability while establishing a culture of transparency that transformed performance.

7. Coaching Leadership

Core approach: Leaders focus on developing individuals' long-term capabilities through guidance and feedback.

When it works best:

- Organizations investing in talent development
- Teams with members at different developmental stages
- Contexts requiring continuous improvement
- Environments valuing knowledge transfer

Limitations:

- Requires significant time investment
- May move too slowly in crisis situations
- Demands excellent interpersonal skills
- Works best with willing, motivated participants

Microsoft CEO Satya Nadella has embodied coaching leadership in transforming the company's culture, emphasizing learning over knowing and creating psychological safety for experimentation.[8] His approach replaced a cutthroat culture with a growth mindset orientation that revitalized the organization.

---

7   Bryce G. Hoffman, *American Icon: Alan Mulally and the Fight to Save Ford Motor Company* (New York: Crown Business, 2012), 123-127.

8   Satya Nadella, *Hit Refresh: The Quest to Rediscover Microsoft's Soul and Imagine a Better Future for Everyone* (New York: HarperBusiness, 2017), 86-89.

Situational Leadership: Adapting Your Approach

While understanding these distinct styles is valuable, truly effective leadership rarely fits perfectly into a single category. Situational leadership, developed by Paul Hersey and Ken Blanchard, recognizes that the optimal approach varies based on team members' readiness level (ability and willingness) for specific tasks.[9]

The situational approach suggests that leaders should adapt their style across four response modes:

1. **Directing** (high direction, low support) for those who lack ability and confidence
2. **Coaching** (high direction, high support) for those with some ability but limited confidence
3. **Supporting** (low direction, high support) for those with ability but wavering commitment
4. **Delegating** (low direction, low support) for those with both ability and commitment

This flexible approach recognizes that even within the same team, different individuals may require different leadership styles based on their development level for specific responsibilities.

Discovering Your Leadership Style

While versatility matters, most leaders have natural tendencies toward certain styles based on personality, values, and experiences. Understanding your default approach helps you leverage your strengths while developing complementary capabilities.

---

9   Paul Hersey and Kenneth H. Blanchard, *Management of Organizational Behavior: Utilizing Human Resources* (Englewood Cliffs, NJ: Prentice Hall, 1982), 150-152.

To identify your natural leadership style, consider these questions:

1. **Decision-making preference**: Do you typically make decisions independently, consultatively, or by consensus?

2. **Communication tendency**: Do you primarily communicate through directives, questions, or inspirational messages?

3. **Feedback approach**: Do you offer structured performance metrics, coaching conversations, or visionary challenges?

4. **Conflict response**: Do you address conflicts through authority, facilitated discussion, or individual conversations?

5. **Change management**: Do you implement change through detailed plans, collaborative processes, or inspiring visions?

Your patterns across these dimensions often reveal your default leadership style. This isn't about labeling yourself, but rather developing self-awareness that enables more intentional choices.

Finding Your Authentic Leadership Voice

While adaptability matters, authenticity remains essential. Research by Bill George and his colleagues at Harvard Business School found that effective leaders don't adopt a theoretical model of leadership but rather develop an authentic approach aligned with their personal values and experiences.[10]

---

10   Bill George, Peter Sims, Andrew N. McLean, and Diana Mayer, "Discovering Your Authentic Leadership," *Harvard Business Review* 85, no. 2 (2007): 129-138.

Authentic leadership doesn't mean rigidly adhering to your natural tendencies regardless of context. Instead, it means adapting your approach in ways that remain true to your core values while meeting the needs of those you lead.

As management scholar Peter Drucker noted, "The most effective leaders are all alike in one crucial way: they don't try to be someone else."[11] Your most powerful leadership emerges when you build on your authentic strengths rather than attempting to adopt an incompatible style that feels forced or artificial.

Developing Style Versatility

While honoring your authentic leadership voice, developing greater versatility across styles creates valuable flexibility. Consider these approaches for expanding your leadership repertoire:

Identify your stretch styles. Which leadership approaches feel least natural but would be most valuable in your context? Focus development efforts on these high-leverage opportunities.

Create deliberate practice opportunities. Look for low-risk situations to experiment with different leadership approaches. For example, if you're naturally directive, practice facilitating a collaborative discussion on a non-critical issue.

Find exemplars to observe. Identify leaders who effectively demonstrate styles different from your own. Notice not just what they do but how they adapt to changing circumstances.

Seek specific feedback. Ask trusted colleagues to observe your

---

11   Peter F. Drucker, *The Effective Executive: The Definitive Guide to Getting the Right Things Done* (New York: HarperBusiness, 2006), 62.

leadership in different situations and provide input on which approaches seem most and least effective.

Develop contextual triggers. Create mental cues that remind you to shift styles when certain conditions arise. For example, "When entering a brainstorming session, I'll switch to a facilitative approach."

The Style Matrix: Matching Approach to Situation

Rather than pursuing a single "best" leadership style, develop the discernment to match your approach to the specific needs of each situation. Consider these contextual factors:

Task complexity: Simple, routine tasks often benefit from more directive leadership, while complex problems may require more collaborative approaches.

Time constraints: Crisis situations typically demand more decisive leadership, while longer-term initiatives allow for more participative processes.

Team capability: Experienced, skilled teams generally respond better to delegative approaches, while developing teams may need more directive guidance.

Organizational culture: Your leadership approach should consider the broader cultural context in which you operate, adapting to work effectively within established norms.

Personal strengths: Your natural capabilities and limitations should inform which approaches you emphasize, particularly in high-pressure situations.

Leadership style isn't about finding the one perfect approach; it's about developing the versatility to meet diverse needs while remaining authentic to your core values and identity.

Final Thoughts: Beyond Style to Substance

While understanding leadership styles provides valuable insight, effectiveness ultimately depends less on style than on substance. The most fundamental leadership question isn't "How do I lead?" but "Why do I lead?"

Your leadership purpose—the positive difference you're committed to making—provides the foundation for authentic leadership that transcends any particular style. When your actions consistently align with your purpose and values, the specific approach you take becomes secondary to the integrity you demonstrate.

As you develop your leadership style, remember that the goal isn't perfection but impact. The measure of leadership isn't found in how closely you adhere to a theoretical model, but in how effectively you help others achieve their potential and purpose.

Chapter 6
Are You Ready to Be a Leader?

Leadership isn't just a position—it's a responsibility, a calling, and a journey of continuous development. Whether you're considering your first leadership role or evaluating your readiness for greater responsibility, this critical question deserves thoughtful consideration: Are you ready to be a leader?

This chapter isn't about discouraging your leadership aspirations but rather about providing a realistic framework to assess and develop your leadership readiness. The goal is to help you enter leadership with clarity about both its challenges and rewards.

The Leadership Readiness Question

Throughout history, some of the most effective leaders initially hesitated to take on leadership roles. Moses protested his inadequacy when called to lead the Israelites. Abraham Lincoln expressed deep doubts about his ability to lead during America's greatest crisis. Even contemporary leaders like Sheryl Sandberg have written about experiencing impostor syndrome despite their significant capabilities.[1]

This hesitation often stems from a healthy recognition of leadership's weight. As John F. Kennedy observed, "Leadership and learning are

---

1   Sheryl Sandberg, *Lean In: Women, Work, and the Will to Lead* (New York: Alfred A. Knopf, 2013), 27-29.

indispensable to each other."[2] The best leaders maintain a learning orientation throughout their careers, recognizing that leadership development is never complete.

Yet leadership readiness isn't about perfection. It's about having sufficient foundation in core competencies while maintaining the humility to keep growing. Let's explore these essential leadership competencies and how to develop them.

The Leadership Readiness Framework

Effective leadership rests on six foundational pillars. Your current capabilities across these dimensions constitute your leadership readiness:

1. Character and Integrity

Leadership begins with who you are rather than what you do. Research by leadership experts James Kouzes and Barry Posner spanning more than 40 years and 30 countries consistently finds that honesty ranks as the most essential leadership quality across cultures, genders, and industries.[3]

Key indicators of readiness:

- You maintain consistent ethical standards regardless of convenience
- Your private actions align with your public statements

---

2   John F. Kennedy, speech prepared for delivery in Dallas the day of his assassination, November 22, 1963.

3   James M. Kouzes and Barry Z. Posner, *The Leadership Challenge: How to Make Extraordinary Things Happen in Organizations,* 6th ed. (Hoboken: Wiley, 2017), 32-33.

- You take responsibility for mistakes rather than deflecting blame
- You speak truth even when it's uncomfortable or unpopular
- You fulfill commitments even when circumstances change

Development opportunities:

- Identify and articulate your core values
- Find accountability partners who will speak honestly about your blind spots
- Practice ethical decision-making by consciously examining choices through multiple moral lenses
- Study ethical frameworks that provide structure for difficult decisions

2. Vision and Strategic Thinking

Leaders see possibilities beyond current reality and chart paths toward preferred futures. While tactical thinking focuses on immediate tasks, strategic thinking connects daily actions to larger purposes.

Key indicators of readiness:

- You naturally consider long-term implications of decisions
- You identify patterns and connections across seemingly unrelated information
- You communicate compelling pictures of future possibilities
- You balance aspirational thinking with practical constraints
- You help others understand how their work contributes to larger goals

Development opportunities:

- Practice scenario planning for different possible futures
- Regularly expose yourself to diverse perspectives and industries
- Set aside dedicated time for reflection beyond daily operations
- Find mentors who demonstrate exceptional strategic thinking
- Study organizations that successfully transformed through clear vision

3. Emotional Intelligence

Leadership inherently involves relationships, making emotional intelligence—the ability to recognize, understand, and manage emotions in yourself and others—an essential capability. Research by Daniel Goleman found that emotional intelligence accounted for 67% of the abilities deemed necessary for effective leadership performance.[4]

Key indicators of readiness:

- You maintain composure during stressful situations
- You recognize how your emotions affect your behavior and decisions
- You accurately read others' emotional states and adapt your approach accordingly
- You build genuine connections across diverse personality types
- You navigate conflicts constructively rather than avoiding or escalating them

---

4   Daniel Goleman, "What Makes a Leader?" *Harvard Business Review* 76, no. 6 (1998): 93-102.

Development opportunities:

- Practice naming your emotions with greater specificity
- Seek feedback about how others experience your emotional responses
- Develop regular reflection practices to increase self-awareness
- Study how emotions influence decision-making and group dynamics
- Build relationships with people quite different from yourself

4. Learning Agility

In rapidly changing environments, learning agility—the ability to learn from experience and apply that learning to new situations—becomes increasingly vital. Research by the Center for Creative Leadership found that learning agility was a stronger predictor of leadership success than IQ, education, or previous job performance.[5]

Key indicators of readiness:

- You actively seek feedback about your performance and impact
- You reflect on experiences to extract meaningful lessons
- You apply insights from one context to solve problems in another
- You demonstrate curiosity about diverse topics beyond your specialty
- You adapt your approach when initial efforts don't succeed

---

5   Michael M. Lombardo and Robert W. Eichinger, *The Leadership Machine* (Minneapolis: Lominger Limited, 2002), 323-324.

Development opportunities:

- Establish regular reflection practices to extract learning from experiences
- Deliberately seek assignments outside your comfort zone
- Develop structured approaches to gather and apply feedback
- Read broadly across disciplines to develop mental models
- Practice reframing failures as learning opportunities

5. Communication and Influence

Leadership effectiveness depends substantially on communication abilities. Even brilliant strategies fail without clear articulation and successful influence. Leadership expert John Kotter notes that transformation efforts often fail because leaders under-communicate the vision by a factor of 10 to 1,000.[6]

Key indicators of readiness:

- You adapt your communication style to different audiences and contexts
- You explain complex ideas in accessible, meaningful terms
- You listen actively rather than waiting to speak
- You articulate compelling reasons for change that resonate emotionally
- You build buy-in through involvement rather than mandate

---

6   John P. Kotter, *Leading Change* (Boston: Harvard Business School Press, 1996), 10-11.

Development opportunities:

- Practice presenting the same content to different audiences
- Record yourself speaking to identify improvement opportunities
- Study persuasive communication across various mediums
- Seek feedback specifically about your listening effectiveness
- Develop storytelling capabilities that connect facts to meaning

6. Execution Excellence

Vision without execution remains merely aspiration. While strategic thinking sets direction, execution excellence transforms plans into reality. Former IBM CEO Louis Gerstner observed that in his experience, "people in the trenches know when things are going well and when they aren't... execution really is the critical part of a successful strategy."[7]

Key indicators of readiness:

- You establish clear, measurable objectives for initiatives
- You develop actionable plans that anticipate obstacles
- You hold yourself and others accountable for commitments
- You make decisions with appropriate speed and conviction
- You maintain focus on priorities despite distractions

---

7   Louis V. Gerstner Jr., *Who Says Elephants Can't Dance? Inside IBM's Historic Turnaround* (New York: HarperBusiness, 2002), 230.

Development opportunities:

- Implement project management disciplines in your current role
- Practice breaking complex objectives into specific actionable steps
- Develop systems for tracking progress against key metrics
- Study how successful initiatives maintain momentum through challenges
- Seek opportunities to lead projects even without formal authority

The Leadership Readiness Assessment

Self-assessment across these six dimensions provides a starting point for understanding your leadership readiness. For each competency, honestly evaluate your current capabilities on a scale from 1 (significant development needed) to 5 (consistent strength).

Remember that leadership readiness doesn't require perfection in all dimensions. Indeed, recognizing your development needs demonstrates the self-awareness essential for growth. What matters most is having sufficient foundation while maintaining commitment to ongoing development.

To gain more objective perspective, consider asking trusted colleagues or mentors to assess your readiness across these same dimensions. The gaps between your self-perception and others' observations often reveal valuable insights about both strengths and blind spots.

Addressing Leadership Fears

Even with strong capabilities, many potential leaders hesitate due to common fears. Acknowledging these concerns directly can help you address them constructively:

Fear of Inadequacy

Many potential leaders worry they lack sufficient knowledge, experience, or capability. This impostor syndrome—the persistent fear of being exposed as a "fraud" despite evidence of competence—affects even accomplished leaders.

Constructive response: Recognize that leadership is always a learning journey. No leader begins with complete readiness, and growth occurs through experience. As leadership expert John Maxwell observes, "The pessimist complains about the wind. The optimist expects it to change. The leader adjusts the sails."[8]

Fear of Failure

Leadership inherently involves risk, making failure a genuine possibility. The public nature of leadership means that failures occur in others' view rather than privately.

Constructive response: Reframe failure as feedback rather than final judgment. Develop resilience by studying how respected leaders rebounded from setbacks. Create contingency plans for major initiatives to reduce catastrophic risk while maintaining appropriate courage. As Winston Churchill noted, "Success is not final, failure is not fatal: it is the courage to continue that counts."[9]

---

8   John C. Maxwell, *The 21 Irrefutable Laws of Leadership: Follow Them and People Will Follow You* (Nashville: Thomas Nelson, 2007), 78.

9   While commonly attributed to Winston Churchill, the exact source of this quote is unclear. The sentiment remains valuable regardless of its precise origin.

Fear of Rejection

Leadership often requires making unpopular decisions and facing criticism. The desire for approval can undermine necessary but difficult choices.

Constructive response: Clarify your values and leadership purpose to provide an anchor during criticism. Distinguish between constructive feedback (which improves performance) and general criticism (which should be considered but not automatically accommodated). Build a support network that provides perspective during challenging periods.

Fear of Responsibility

Leadership carries accountability for outcomes that depend partly on others' performance. This responsibility can feel overwhelming, particularly in challenging circumstances.

Constructive response: Develop systems for appropriate delegation and monitoring. Clarify which responsibilities you can directly control versus those you can only influence. Create advisory relationships with more experienced leaders who can provide guidance during difficult decisions.

Finding Your Leadership Path

Leadership readiness often develops gradually through progressive experiences. Consider these stepping stones that build capacity while providing valuable learning:

Lead projects before leading people. Project leadership develops many core capabilities with somewhat lower stakes than people leadership. Volunteer for initiatives that stretch your capabilities while providing concrete deliverables.

Seek informal leadership opportunities. Look for chances to influence without authority: lead committees, coordinate volunteer efforts, or serve as team representative. These experiences develop persuasion skills essential for formal leadership.

Find mentors at your target level. Build relationships with leaders in positions similar to those you aspire to reach. Their perspective can help you understand the real (versus imagined) challenges of specific leadership roles.

Create developmental assignments. Identify specific experiences that would strengthen your leadership readiness, then proactively seek them. Sometimes lateral moves that provide new capabilities prove more valuable than vertical promotions.

Start small before scaling up. Leading smaller teams or initiatives allows you to develop capabilities before applying them at larger scale. Each expansion provides new learning while building on established strengths.

The Leadership Launch Plan

Once you've assessed your readiness and addressed key concerns, create a concrete plan for your leadership development:

1. Clarify your leadership purpose. Articulate why you want to lead and what positive difference you hope to make. This purpose provides direction and sustains motivation during challenges.
2. Identify your next leadership frontier. Based on your current capabilities and aspirations, what specific leadership role or challenge represents your appropriate next step?

3. Create your development plan. For each key competency, identify specific actions to strengthen your capabilities. Focus particularly on dimensions most relevant to your target role.
4. Build your support system. Leadership development doesn't happen in isolation. Identify mentors, coaches, peers, and resources that will support your growth.
5. Establish reflection practices. Create regular intervals to assess your progress, extract learning from experiences, and refine your approach.

Leadership Readiness Is a Journey, Not a Destination

Even the most experienced leaders continue developing throughout their careers. The question isn't whether you're completely ready—no one ever is—but whether you have sufficient foundation while maintaining the humility to keep growing.

As management expert Peter Drucker noted, "The best way to predict the future is to create it."[10] Your leadership readiness isn't primarily about meeting some external standard, but about developing the capabilities to create the future you envision—for yourself, your organization, and those you're privileged to lead.

Leadership isn't promised to be easy, but it offers unique opportunities to create positive impact beyond what you could achieve individually. When approached with the right mindset, leadership becomes not just a responsibility but a profound source of meaning, growth, and contribution.

---

10   Peter F. Drucker, *The Ecological Vision: Reflections on the American Condition* (New York: Routledge, 1993), 122.

As you consider your leadership readiness, remember that the most important qualification isn't perfection but purpose—a genuine commitment to making a positive difference through your influence. With this foundation, your leadership journey can begin whenever you choose to take that first courageous step.

Chapter 7
Putting It All Together: Your Leadership Journey

Throughout this book, we've explored various dimensions of successful leadership: clarifying goals, communicating effectively, leading across generations, implementing the 5 Keys to winning in business, understanding leadership styles, and assessing your leadership readiness. Now it's time to integrate these elements into a cohesive approach for your leadership journey.

The Integrated Leadership Model

Leadership isn't about mastering isolated skills but developing an integrated approach where each element reinforces the others. Consider how the core components we've discussed work together:

- Clear leadership goals (Chapter 1) provide direction for your communication efforts (Chapter 2)
- Understanding generational dynamics (Chapter 3) helps you adapt your leadership style (Chapter 5)
- The 5 Keys framework (Chapter 4) builds the foundation for leadership readiness (Chapter 6)

Successful leaders don't compartmentalize these elements but weave them together into a consistent, authentic approach. As Harvard Business School professor Nancy Koehn observed after studying exceptional leaders across centuries, "Great leaders are made, not born, and they are made through a lifetime of development that includes critical setbacks and failures, as well as personal resilience, courage, and introspection."[1]

Your Leadership Philosophy Statement

A leadership philosophy statement articulates your core beliefs about leadership and how you intend to practice it. This living document serves multiple purposes:

- Provides a compass for decision-making during challenging situations
- Creates accountability for consistent leadership behavior
- Communicates your approach to those you lead
- Establishes a foundation for ongoing reflection and refinement

While there's no single correct format, effective leadership philosophy statements typically address:

1. Your leadership purpose - Why you lead and what difference you hope to make
2. Your core values - The principles that guide your decisions and actions
3. Your leadership approach - How you typically engage with those you lead
4. Your expectations - What others can consistently expect from you
5. Your growth commitments - How you will continue developing as a leader

---

1   Nancy F. Koehn, *Forged in Crisis: The Power of Courageous Leadership in Turbulent Times* (New York: Scribner, 2017), 3.

Here's a sample leadership philosophy statement that illustrates these elements:

My leadership purpose is to build high-performing teams that deliver exceptional results while developing each member's capabilities and confidence. I lead through four core values: integrity in all interactions, courage to address challenges directly, curiosity about diverse perspectives, and commitment to both excellence and well-being.

My leadership approach balances clear direction with collaborative problem-solving. I provide context and purpose for initiatives, establish measurable outcomes, and give teams appropriate autonomy in execution while remaining accessible for guidance and support.

Those I lead can expect consistent, timely communication; honest, constructive feedback; recognition for contributions; and advocacy for their development. I'll acknowledge mistakes, share credit for successes, and make decisions transparently based on both data and values.

To continue growing as a leader, I commit to seeking regular feedback, reflecting on experiences, studying diverse leadership perspectives, and adapting my approach as team needs and organizational contexts evolve.

This example demonstrates specificity while maintaining flexibility for adaptation across situations. Your leadership philosophy should reflect your authentic voice and unique perspective rather than generic platitudes.

Take time to draft your own leadership philosophy statement, then refine it through reflection and feedback from trusted colleagues. Revisit and revise it periodically as your leadership journey progresses.

Your 30-60-90 Day Leadership Development Plan

While long-term growth matters, concrete short-term actions build momentum and establish productive patterns. A 30-60-90 day plan provides structure for your immediate development priorities.

First 30 Days: Foundation

- Complete a thorough self-assessment across the six leadership readiness dimensions (Chapter 6)
- Request feedback from 3-5 trusted colleagues about your leadership strengths and growth areas
- Identify the highest-leverage development opportunity based on this input
- Draft your leadership philosophy statement
- Select one leadership book aligned with your primary development area

Days 31-60: Skill Building

- Establish a specific learning objective for your target development area
- Create deliberate practice opportunities focused on this objective
- Identify a mentor or coach with expertise in your focus area
- Implement one new leadership practice from each chapter of this book
- Begin a leadership journal to capture insights and track progress

Days 61-90: Application and Feedback

- Apply your developing skills in a specific leadership initiative
- Request focused feedback on your progress in your target area
- Revise your leadership philosophy based on new

insights
- Establish a peer learning group for ongoing development
- Create your longer-term leadership development roadmap

This structured approach prevents the common pattern where initial motivation fades without concrete action. Each step builds on previous progress while establishing habits that support continuous growth.

Measuring Leadership Success

Traditional metrics like profit margins and productivity certainly matter, but comprehensive leadership assessment requires broader measurement. Consider these additional dimensions:

Team Development Metrics

- Skill acquisition and career progression among team members
- Internal promotion rates from your team
- Employee engagement and satisfaction scores
- Retention of high-performing team members
- Knowledge sharing and collaboration indicators

Organizational Impact Metrics

- Innovation and improvement initiatives generated
- Cross-functional collaboration effectiveness
- Organizational reputation and brand perception
- Customer satisfaction and loyalty
- Sustainability of results over time

Personal Growth Metrics

- Expansion of leadership responsibilities
- Feedback quality and trajectory
- Ability to adapt to changing circumstances
- Work-life integration and personal well-being
- Development of others' leadership capabilities

As productivity expert Peter Drucker observed, "What gets measured gets managed."[2] By establishing measurement across these dimensions, you create accountability for holistic leadership development rather than focusing exclusively on financial outcomes.

Leadership Legacy Planning

While immediate success matters, truly great leaders think beyond their tenure to the lasting impact they hope to create. Legacy planning isn't just for the end of your career—it should inform your leadership approach from the beginning.

Leadership expert Tim Elmore defines legacy as "what continues to grow once you're gone."[3] Consider these questions to clarify your desired leadership legacy:

1. What lasting difference do you want your leadership to make for:

    - The people you've led?
    - The organization you've served?
    - The broader community or industry?

---

2   While commonly attributed to Peter Drucker, this phrase may have originated with other management thinkers. Regardless of its source, the principle remains valid.

3   Tim Elmore, *Habitudes: Images That Form Leadership Habits and Attitudes* (Atlanta: Growing Leaders, 2013), 45.

2. What leadership principles or practices do you hope others will carry forward?
3. How will success be defined 5-10 years after your leadership role ends?
4. What systems or cultural elements should outlast your direct involvement?
5. Which emerging leaders will you specifically develop to extend your impact?

Your answers to these questions help prioritize how you invest your leadership energy and resources. As organizational psychologist Adam Grant notes, "The meaning of your work isn't what you do; it's the impact you have on others. Leaders have a responsibility to act now with future generations in mind."[4]

Continuous Leadership Renewal

Leadership effectiveness requires ongoing renewal to prevent stagnation and burnout. Research on sustainable leadership from the Center for Creative Leadership identifies four critical dimensions of renewal:[5]

Physical Renewal Leadership demands significant energy, making physical well-being a professional necessity rather than a personal luxury. Establish sustainable practices for sleep, nutrition, exercise, and recovery to maintain the stamina leadership requires.

Mental Renewal Prevent cognitive staleness by exposing yourself to diverse perspectives and disciplines. Read widely, engage with people

---

4   Adam Grant, *Give and Take: A Revolutionary Approach to Success* (New York: Penguin Books, 2014), 268.

5   Ellen Van Velsor, Cynthia D. McCauley, and Marian N. Ruderman, eds., *The Center for Creative Leadership Handbook of Leadership Development,* 3rd ed. (San Francisco: Jossey-Bass, 2010), 135-137.

outside your usual circles, and periodically step back from daily operations to think strategically.

Emotional Renewal Leadership often involves absorbing others' concerns while projecting confidence despite uncertainty. Create practices for emotional processing, whether through trusted conversations, reflective writing, creative expression, or other approaches aligned with your preferences.

Purpose Renewal Even meaningful work can lose its motivating power without conscious reconnection to purpose. Regularly engage with the impact of your work through customer interactions, success stories, or direct exposure to the difference your organization makes.

Leadership consultant Brené Brown emphasizes, "We can't give what we don't have. We can't lead without courage, empathy, and resilience. And we can't sustain those qualities without renewal."[6]

Embracing Leadership as a Journey

As we conclude this exploration of successful leadership, remember that leadership excellence isn't a destination but a continuous journey of growth and impact. Even the most accomplished leaders remain works in progress, constantly learning, adapting, and developing.

The path isn't always linear or predictable. You'll experience setbacks along with successes, confusion alongside clarity. This variability isn't evidence of failure but the natural terrain of meaningful leadership development.

---

6   Brené Brown, *Dare to Lead: Brave Work. Tough Conversations. Whole Hearts.* (New York: Random House, 2018), 271.

Leadership author Max De Pree captured this perspective: "Leadership is much more an art, a belief, a condition of the heart, than a set of things to do. The visible signs of artful leadership are expressed, ultimately, in its practice."[7]

The practices outlined throughout this book provide structure for your development, but the art of leadership emerges through their authentic application in your unique context. As you integrate these elements into your approach, your leadership voice becomes increasingly distinct and impactful.

Your Leadership Invitation

Leadership isn't reserved for those with certain titles, personalities, or backgrounds. It's available to anyone willing to develop the necessary capabilities while serving others with purpose and integrity.

Your leadership journey might begin with leading yourself well, then expand to projects, teams, organizations, or movements. Each context provides opportunities to apply the principles we've explored while developing new dimensions of your leadership capacity.

The world desperately needs effective, ethical leaders at every level—people who combine clear purpose with practical skills to address challenges and create positive change. Your willingness to embrace this responsibility represents a significant contribution in itself.

As anthropologist Margaret Mead observed, "Never doubt that a small group of thoughtful, committed citizens can change the world; indeed, it's the only thing that ever has."[8] Your leadership journey

---

7   Max De Pree, *Leadership Is an Art* (New York: Currency, 2004), 11.
8   While commonly attributed to Margaret Mead, there is some debate about the exact origin of this quote. The sentiment aligns with her published works and public statements regardless of its precise source.

creates ripples far beyond what you can initially see or measure.

I encourage you to begin or continue this journey with both confidence and humility—confidence in your capacity to grow and contribute, coupled with the humility to keep learning throughout the process. The path of leadership offers not just achievement but profound meaning through positive impact on others' lives and work.

What will your next step be?

RESOURCES

The following resources will help you continue your leadership development journey beyond this book. They are organized by category to help you focus on specific aspects of leadership that most interest you or align with your current development needs.

Leadership Books

On Leadership Fundamentals

- Kouzes, James M., and Barry Z. Posner. *The Leadership Challenge: How to Make Extraordinary Things Happen in Organizations.* 6th ed. San Francisco: Jossey-Bass, 2017.
- Maxwell, John C. T*he 21 Irrefutable Laws of Leadership: Follow Them and People Will Follow You.* Revised ed. Nashville: Thomas Nelson, 2007.
- Brown, Brené. *Dare to Lead: Brave Work. Tough Conversations. Whole Hearts.* New York: Random House, 2018.
- Sinek, Simon. *Start with Why: How Great Leaders Inspire Everyone to Take Action.* New York: Portfolio, 2009.

On Leadership Communication

- Grenny, Joseph, Kerry Patterson, David Maxfield, Ron McMillan, and Al Switzler. *Crucial Conversations: Tools for Talking When Stakes Are High.* 2nd ed. New York: McGraw-Hill, 2012.

- Scott, Kim. *Radical Candor: Be a Kick-Ass Boss Without Losing Your Humanity.* New York: St. Martin's Press, 2017.
- Heath, Chip, and Dan Heath. *Made to Stick: Why Some Ideas Survive and Others Die.* New York: Random House, 2007.

On Leading Different Generations

- Chou, Sabrina Yvonne. *Millennials to Mainstream: A Generational Bridge to the Future Workplace.* Hoboken: Wiley, 2022.
- Stillman, David, and Jonah Stillman. *Gen Z @ Work: How the Next Generation Is Transforming the Workplace.* New York: HarperBusiness, 2017.
- Murphy, Mark. *Generation Z: Understanding the Next Generational Workforce.* Leadership IQ, 2020.

On Leadership Style and Authenticity

- Goleman, Daniel, Richard Boyatzis, and Annie McKee. *Primal Leadership: Unleashing the Power of Emotional Intelligence.* Boston: Harvard Business Review Press, 2013.
- George, Bill, and Peter Sims. *True North: Discover Your Authentic Leadership.* San Francisco: Jossey-Bass, 2007.
- Kahnweiler, Jennifer B. *The Introverted Leader: Building on Your Quiet Strength.* 2nd ed. Oakland: Berrett-Koehler Publishers, 2018.

On Leadership Character and Integrity

- Cloud, Henry. *Integrity: The Courage to Meet the*

Demands of Reality. New York: HarperCollins, 2006.
- Arbinger Institute. *Leadership and Self-Deception: Getting Out of the Box.* San Francisco: Berrett-Koehler Publishers, 2010.
- Johnson, Craig E. *Meeting the Ethical Challenges of Leadership: Casting Light or Shadow.* 6th ed. Thousand Oaks: SAGE Publications, 2018.

Leadership Podcasts

- "Leadership Now" with Andy Stanley
- "At the Table with Patrick Lencioni"
- "HBR IdeaCast" by Harvard Business Review
- "The John Maxwell Leadership Podcast"
- "Coaching for Leaders" with Dave Stachowiak
- "Lead to Win" with Michael Hyatt
- "The Ed Mylett Show"

Online Leadership Resources

Leadership Assessments

- VIA Character Strengths Survey - Free assessment of character strengths
- CliftonStrengths Assessment - Identifies your top natural talents
- DiSC Profile - Communication and behavioral styles assessment
- Leadership Circle Profile - 360-degree leadership effectiveness assessment

Leadership Development Organizations

- Center for Creative Leadership - Research-based leadership development

- John Maxwell Team - Leadership training and certification
- Society for Human Resource Management - Resources on leadership and people management
- Leadership IQ - Research-driven leadership tools and training

Leadership Articles and Resources

- Harvard Business Review Leadership Section
- McKinsey & Company Leadership Insights
- MIT Sloan Management Review
- Stanford Social Innovation Review

Leadership Development Programs

Executive Education (Short Courses)

- Harvard Business School Executive Education
- Stanford Graduate School of Business Executive Programs
- Wharton Executive Education
- Center for Creative Leadership Leadership Development Program

Online Leadership Courses

- Coursera: "Leading People and Teams" specialization by University of Michigan
- LinkedIn Learning: "Becoming a Leader" learning path
- edX: "Leadership Essentials" professional certificate by Dartmouth
- Udemy: "Leadership: Practical Leadership Skills" by Chris Croft

Leadership Networks and Communities

- Young Presidents' Organization (YPO) - Global leadership community for chief executives
- Vistage - Executive coaching and peer advisory groups
- National Association of Women Business Owners - Support for women entrepreneurs and business owners
- International Leadership Association - Global network for leadership scholars and practitioners

Scripture Resources for Leadership

- Blackaby, Henry T., and Richard Blackaby. *Spiritual Leadership: Moving People on to God's Agenda.* Revised ed. Nashville: B&H Books, 2011.
- Wilkes, C. Gene. *Jesus on Leadership: Timeless Wisdom on Servant Leadership.* Carol Stream: Tyndale House Publishers, 1998.
- Hybels, Bill. *Courageous Leadership.* Grand Rapids: Zondervan, 2009.
- Blanchard, Ken, and Phil Hodges. *Lead Like Jesus: Lessons from the Greatest Leadership Role Model of All Time.* Nashville: Thomas Nelson, 2008.

Digital Tools for Leaders

Productivity and Organization

- Asana - Project management and team coordination
- Trello - Visual organization of projects and tasks
- Evernote - Note-taking and information organization
- Todoist - Task management and prioritization

Communication and Collaboration

- Slack - Team communication and collaboration
- Microsoft Teams - Integrated communication and file sharing
- Zoom - Video conferencing with recording capabilities
- Loom - Video messaging for asynchronous communication

Learning and Development

- Blinkist - Summaries of business and leadership books
- MasterClass - Leadership courses from world-class experts
- Audible - Audiobooks for learning during commutes
- Pocket - Save articles for later reading and reference

Connect With Me

I'm passionate about helping emerging and established leaders reach their full potential. For additional resources, speaking engagements, or leadership coaching:

- Website: Iambarbarapalmer.com
- Email: info@iambarbarapalmer.com
- LinkedIn: @iambarbarapalmer.com
- Instagram: @iambarbarapalmer.com
- YouTube: @iambarbarapalmer.com

About the Author

Dr. Barbara Palmer is a world-renowned speaker, pastor, coach, best-selling author, philanthropist, and award-winning entrepreneur. She is the owner and CEO of Kingdom Kare Childcare Center, a nationally accredited program, as well as the founder of the profitable nonprofit organization Kingdom Kare Inc. and Palmer Consulting LLC.

With over 30 years of expertise in corporate, nonprofit, and financial management, Dr. Palmer has successfully written grants that have generated over $5 million for her nonprofit and consulting clients. Her work focuses on coaching and consulting business owners worldwide, equipping them with strategies for organizational development, nonprofit leadership, and sustainable growth. Her dynamic trainings cover topics such as grant writing, business establishment, capacity building, and personal empowerment.

Dr. Palmer is the author of the autobiographical best-seller I AM: One Woman's Journey to Find Healing After Loss, The Barbara Palmer Story, detailing her remarkable path to healing and success. She is also the creator of the highly anticipated 5 Keys book series, which outlines her proven strategies for personal and business growth.

Key Accomplishments

- First in her family to become a millionaire.
- Recognized in Marquis Who's Who.
- Featured in The Baltimore Times and The Motherlode Magazine.
- Received the Michelle Obama "100 Women Making a Difference" Award.
- Winner of a national grant from the American Heart Association Accelerator Program.
- Honored with the Dr. Thelma Daily Award by Delta Sigma Theta for her work with teen mothers.
- Delivered speeches to audiences of over 5,000 worldwide.

Education

Dr. Palmer holds a BA in Bank Finance, a BA in Divinity, an MA in Pastoral Counseling, an MA in Early Childhood Education with a minor in Psychology, and a PhD in Humane Letters and Cultural Competency. She is also certified in Human Rights and Mental Health First Aid.

Popular Speaking Topics

- I Am Barbara Palmer: One Woman's Journey to Finding Healing
- Leading Without Fear: 7 Ways to Unlock, Become, and Soar
- Awakening: Moving from Stagnation to Activation
- Toxicity Stinks: 5 Keys to Remove the Odor from Your Mind
- The Profitable Nonprofit: 3 Keys to Finding Funding to Sustain Your Organization

- Money, Money, Money: How to Leverage Connections for Resources
- Royal Kids: Starting a Six-Figure Childcare Business
- Let Her Speak: Turning Your Mess into a Message

Personal Life and Ministry

Dr. Palmer serves alongside her husband, Apostle Antonio Palmer, at Kingdom Celebration Center in Gambrills, Maryland. Together, they have dedicated their lives to ministry, business, and empowering their community.

Dr. Palmer is also the founder of Kingdom Kare, Inc., employing over 55 staff and working with a volunteer base of more than 30 people to empower children, youth, and families through education and support programs.

Residing in Maryland with her husband of 31 years, Dr. Palmer cherishes her family time with her children and grandchildren while continuing to inspire others through her speaking engagements, workshops, and one-on-one coaching.

www.ingramcontent.com/pod-product-compliance
Lightning Source LLC
Chambersburg PA
CBHW061704120626
46550CB00003B/1086